In My Father's Footsteps

In My Father's Footsteps

Robin A. Edgar

Landrum, South Carolina

Published by
Tree House Enterprises
www.treehouseonline.net

(c) Copyright 2024 by Robin A. Edgar
All rights reserved. No part of this book may be reproduced in any form or by any electronic or mechanical means, including information storage and retrieval systems, without permission in writing from the author.

Library of Congress Control Number: 2024900861

Cover and book design by
David Adelman

ISBN: 978-0-9723770-4-1 (pbk. : alk. paper)

Library of Congress Cataloging-in-Publication Data

Summary: In My Father's Footsteps offers individuals examples of how to recall significant memories and celebrate the individuals and incidents that shaped their lives.

1. Reminiscing. 2. Self awareness

I. Title.

Printed and bound in the United States of America

To my father, Jacob William Babich, who taught me to build community by helping people. His motto was: I wondered why somebody didn't do something. Then I realized that I am somebody.

My dad, Jack Babich

Contents

Introduction. xi
Hey Pete! 1
Me, My Dad, and Sauerkraut 9
A Day at the Races 15
Daddy Longlegs 23
The Importance of Community 29
The West Delray Democratic Club. 35
Building Friendships with Advice. 43
Bipartisan Politics. 49
Use It Up 55
Pieces of String and Pennies from Heaven 61
Leaving a Legacy 67
Finding Memories to Footsteps 73
Acknowledgements 85
About the Author 87

Introduction

With 15 minutes to get bathed, dressed, coiffed, and out the door, I dove into my bath feet first. Seconds later, I jumped out scalded and screaming. A minor dispute with the wonderful man—and I emphasize man—that I married is the temperature setting on our hot water heater. While he opts to singe the top layer of his skin in the shower, I prefer to gently soak in warm water. Anyway, back to my story. Hopping about to cool my heels, the sopping-wet footprints on the cotton bath mat stopped me in my tracks.

They reminded me of the impressions my father's footsteps left in the sand when we walked on the beach –something he did not enjoy as much as I did. That was because he had such a hard time getting the sand out from between his hammer toes that seemed perpetually crossed over each other for good luck.

Ever thankful that I did not inherit those crooked toes, I was surprised by the crescent-shaped imprints before me. They clearly said that, as much as I adored my mother and hoped to be like her when I grew up, I had also inherited some of my father's traits. Thinking about some of the things about dear old Dad that drove me crazy, like the way he picked imaginary lint off of my clothes when he wanted to change the subject, or how his poor business sense impacted our family, I was relieved to assess that I was not entirely like him. My penchant, however, for solving people's problems, whether they asked me to or not, was indeed just like Dad. If the saying is true that you become what you look at, I wondered how else I had become like my dad over the years.

As my bath grew cooler, I mused about the impact his genes as well as his example had on my life. Wasn't it my good fortune to inherit his ability to make friends with complete strangers? Wasn't his perpetual optimism a trait that I often used to my advantage? The more I thought about it, the more I realized how proud I was to follow in his footsteps.

My first book, *In My Mother's Kitchen: An Introduction to the Healing Power of Reminiscence*, celebrates my mother – what she meant to me and taught me by her example. If you never knew your father, you may have had other relatives or people who had a great influence on you. I hope my stories in this book will encourage you to recall the memories of the significant people and events in your life. At the end of each story, the "In His Footsteps" section shows you by example how, reflecting on those people and events, reveals how they can shape who you are.

Hey Pete!

Dad and his friend Sammy Gensler

When I was a little girl, I loved to tag along with my father, half running and tripping to keep up with his long-legged strides. Inevitably, he would call out, "Hey Pete!" to someone and they would stop to talk to him. Shy as I was back then, that was my cue to disappear behind his spindly legs in hopes no one would ask me my name or how old I was. This happened so often that it made me think that my father knew just about everyone in our small Brooklyn neighborhood. What amazed me even more was that all of his friends were named Pete!

When I was older, I finally asked him why he called everyone Pete. He laughed and, "If I can't remember someone's name, or even if they are a stranger and I just need directions, it seems like everyone will answer to Pete." That may have been a trick he used to get people's attention but, the more I learned about my father, the more I saw that he only needed a short conversation with someone to call them his friend. This character trait worked well for him in many ways, particularly in his political and community service, but was conversely the cause, in part, of the downfall of the family business.

After his father died, Dad ran a family delicatessen located in downtown Manhattan. It did a thriving business and, during the lunch hour, people lined up two or three deep at the counter, waiting for a seated patron to leave so they could sit down for a quick Coke and pastrami on rye before returning to work. Business began to wane, however, when the Horn and Hardart automat opened and you could get your lunch in much less time. The food may not have been so good, but you did not have to stand in line and your sandwich was waiting for you as long as you fed quarters in the slot.

According to my mother, who had married him shortly after the automat opened, he kept the failing business open saying, "My friends won't leave me; they'll come back." Confident that all of the customers he had "befriended" over the years would not let him go under, he went further and further in to debt until he was forced to close the deli. With two young ones at home, my mother, a professional seamstress and pattern maker, opened a bridal shop to bring in the money to pay the bills and my dad stayed home with us kids until he could find a job. As young as I was, I can still remember him singing to me as he fed me in my high chair near the small kitchen window.

Finally, my father got a job working as the headwaiter for the Turf and Surf Field Club at Belmont Racetrack and later at the restaurant at the Aqueduct Racetrack. He also worked for catered affairs on the weekends. My mother closed her bridal shop and we moved to a garden apartment in the neighborhood in Queens, not far from her sister and one of her brothers and their families, and much closer to Dad's new job at the racetrack. Mom set up shop at home as seamstress so she could be there for us kids.

My dad never lost his penchant for friends, which knew no social or racial boundaries. He occasionally brought a co-worker home with him before heading to work at a catered affair that evening. My dad explained that his "friend" worked with him during the day as a bus boy at the racetrack and lived too far away to go home and take a shower before going on to the catering night job that night. Apparently, my dad was teaching him how to be a waiter so he could make more money to provide for his family. A Puerto Rican, he spoke little English, but you could see the gratitude in his eyes when my mother gave him a fresh towel and a bar of soap to use in the bathroom of our small five-room apartment. Living in an all-white neighborhood, I was fascinated to meet someone from another culture, especially someone who spoke another language. Looking back, I am amazed that my dad was able to communicate with that fellow and to find that simple, yet significant way to help him.

In His Footsteps

Probably influenced my father's example and ability to strike up a conversation and resulting friendship with every "Pete" he came across, I often think that I was born with an extra chromosome that compels me to find the good in and to befriend everyone I meet. Like my father, I "adopted" a young African woman who had come to this country as a political refugee. Once she became a U.S. citizen, I helped her raise the funds to bring her parents here to safety as legal immigrants.

·

Me, My Dad, and Sauerkraut

Whenever I was pregnant, I didn't crave the usual watermelon, ice cream, or pickles. For me, there was just one had-to-have food: sauerkraut. To assure in-stant gratification, I would buy the type that came in plastic bags so, af-ter loading the groceries in my car, I could rip open the zip lock seal and dive in with the plastic fork that I kept in my glove compartment just for that purpose. Perhaps it was the high calcium content that this sweet, tangy treat pro-vided that fueled my yen. Eating sauerkraut also brought me a sense of comfort – and has since I was a little girl.

After my mother's critical illnesses sapped their savings, my father took on more work to make ends meet. After he was done with his day job as headwaiter, he drove a cab in the evenings. He still also served at catered affairs on weekends. Any time with my dad was therefore precious, like when he took me to a baseball game at Shea Stadium. Although I knew very little about the game, I certainly looked forward to our time together. Even if I did not understand what was going on at the diamond, I knew exactly what to expect when Dad whistled to one of the hot dog vendors swimming through the waves of fans. He would beckon him over with a handful of dollar bills and I would hold my hands out in anticipation of receiving the special treat. I would eagerly ingest the sauerkraut and brown mustard topping and only take a bite or two of the meat and then hand over the leftovers for my dad to finish.

As a teenager, I often spent my babysitting money on a train ride on the Long Island Railroad to Play Land where my friends and I would go to the concession stand for hot dogs after the rides. Once I made my purchase, I would go straight over to the long wooden condiment tables with stainless steel bins containing relish, onions, and my favorite – sauerkraut. Piling as much of my beloved kraut that my hotdog platform could hold, I would devour the contents of the cardboard container, then return to fill it with another mound of kraut and mustard for dessert.

In His Footsteps

Today, I love watching baseball, but I no longer eat hot dogs or have an excuse to keep a fork in my glove compartment. I do, however, make my own sauerkraut and there is always a glass jar of it lurking in the back of the fridge if I need a hit. Some habits never die, but at least this one is healthy.

A Day at the Races

To get away from the heat and to find ways to occupy two little girls who were home from school for three months, my mother and dad would pack us up the old Plymouth and drive out to spend the summer at the Jefferson Hotel, an old hunting lodge converted into inexpensive one-bedroom efficiency apartments in Rockaway Beach. Since my dad worked the summer racing venue in Saratoga during the week, he only joined us on weekends. When he was with us, he took full advantage of those times, dancing at the patio parties, playing poker, or going fishing with the menfolk. We had a wonderful time there for many summers and forged lasting friendships with many of the other families that stayed there.

One family in particular, the Genslers, rented the apartment next door to us on the ground level. The father, Sammy, played poker and went fishing with my Dad on weekends. My mother and his wife, Martha, became fast friends, enjoying the respite when we kids paraded down the block for a day at the beach, giving them time to do laundry or even get in a quick game of

Mahjong or Canasta before preparing dinner. Although their eldest son, Joel, was much older than my sister and I, their younger son, Peter, became a constant playmate and, to this day, has been the brother I never had.

I asked Dad's old friend, Sammy, who lived to 103 with all his faculties intact, to share a memory about my dad. He smiled and related the following story about the day they went to the Belmont Raceway, where my dad was the headwaiter at the clubhouse restaurant when Aqueduct was closed.

It was about 1960 when he took me to Belmont. What amazed me was that he knew everybody and everybody knew him. We went into the clubhouse through the kitchen door without being stopped by the Pinkerton security guards. They barely looked at us as we walked right through. Once we were inside, your father turned to me and said, "Stay right here and, when I come back, I'll tell you who to bet on." Then he walked over to a group of people and they conversed for a bit before parting to different places, I suppose to get information. Some went to the stables to talk to trainers and others to the clubhouse boxes to talk to the owners. When they reconvened, they put their heads together and hashed out, sometimes loudly, sometimes in whispers, which horse was the most likely to win. Then your father told me which horse to bet on.

Now I was a $2 bettor and your dad was a $100 bettor. When I went to the $2 window, I was sometimes shut out because the line was so long that they closed the betting before I could get my money down. There was no line at the $100 window, so your dad was always able to get his bet in. At the end of the day, I won $35, which I thought was wonderful, and your dad won a couple of hundred dollars. He had such confidence in the advice of his friends, which worked for us that day, but he didn't always get the right information every time.

That was a good day for my dad but, as Sammy said, it wasn't always the case. My mom once confided in me how my dad often spent his paycheck betting on the losing horse that his friends insisted was a sure thing. She said he just couldn't resist a tip from someone carrying a wad of winnings in his pockets, and she learned to squirrel away her earnings for the rainy days ahead.

In His Footsteps

My dad used to take us kids to the races from time to time and he shared some of the tricks of the trade he had learned from his friends. I had never applied my dad's sure-win formula until recently, when I went to the annual Steeple Chase in Tryon for the first time. For one, I knew to look for the horse that had been winning recently because they usually had a fire in their belly from those conquests. And, since he had emphasized to not just pick only the horse that had won the most money, I selected the one that had been consistently winning all along – even if the total winnings were less than that of others that won one or two big purses. To my delight, I actually came out ahead, winning six out of seven. In the end, I knew it was more luck than formula, but it was a great way to celebrate my dad.

Daddy Longlegs

Dad in his twenties

I'm not exaggerating when I say my father's legs were long. They were skinny, too. And he loved to dance! I imagine that all three characteristics earned him the nickname "Daddy Longlegs."

Always on his feet, Dad continued to work long hours as a maître d' for various racetrack restaurants during the week and as a waiter for caterers on weekends. On Sunday afternoons when he wasn't working, he was usually stretched out on the couch, napping. Who could blame him?

On the rare evenings when he was home, the four of us sat together on the couch to watch TV. Everyone had their designated spot—my mom on one end so she could use the light from the table lamp as she hand-stitched hems or beads on garments for her customers, and Dad on the opposite side of the couch next to the end table where he stashed his favorite snacks (dried figs and a large Hershey bar). He usually propped his poor tired feet up on the coffee table. My sister and I occupied the middle section, me watching my mom's dressmaking expertise and my sister eyeing Dad's milk chocolate bar until he broke off two little squares, one for her and one for me.

As we watched Million Dollar Movie or The Ed Sullivan Show, whenever any dance music came on, Dad's resting feet came alive again. He would grab my hand or my sister's to dance, often with our toes on his feet as he fox trotted or waltzed us around the living room like Fred Astaire and Ginger Rogers.

I also have vivid memories of him dancing when we vacationed during the summer months at the Jefferson Hotel in Rockaway Beach. When he was off from work at the racetrack in Saratoga, he was able to join us at the Saturday night dance parties. The other residents cheered him as they called out, "Go Daddy Longlegs! Go!" He loved to entertain the crowd with his fancy improvisational steps.

In His Footsteps

There's no way to know for sure how I acquired my own love of dance. Perhaps I inherited the same dancing gene that my dad had. What I do know is, every time I get out on the dance floor, albeit with much shorter legs (my sister was the lucky one to get his long, skinny legs), I celebrate those times that Daddy Longlegs and I danced together. Many years ago, I came up with the idea for a weekly "Date Night" for my husband and I to put on oldies music and cut the rug in our own living room.

The Importance
of Community

After my parents retired, they moved to a condominium complex in Delray Beach, Florida called Village of Orioles. There, my dad continued to capitalize on his ability to make friends. Taking after his father who told him, "When somebody comes to you for help, you should try to help them," he lived out his sunset years by the credo that was summarized by a quote by Lily Tomlin on a plaque displayed on the wall in his office:

"I always wondered why somebody doesn't do something about that. Then I realized I was somebody."

After moving there, he noticed that recent westward expansion on Atlantic Avenue had left the medians of that major thoroughfare devoid of vegetation and littered with debris. Deciding something had to be done, he single-handedly campaigned to beautify West Delray. At first, he went up and down the avenue himself, collecting discarded cans, rubber tires, and other trash. Then he brokered a deal with the Palm Beach County Commissioners that, if he raised $10,000 to hire professional laborers to do the planting, the Parks and Recreation Department would provide landscaping plans, and the County would maintain the new vegetation. He also enlisted the help of the county engineering office to get a permit from the Florida Department of Transportation.

Before long, other residents got involved and SidneyKutrick of Kings Point volunteered to assist him. Organizing resident volunteers to clean up the litter, they raised more than $120,000 from the Atlantic Avenue developers, merchants, and citizens. In addition, six local nurseries donated hundreds of plants, mostly trees and shrubs, to fill the median strips. Dad was then able to convince the county Parks and Recreation department to provide the irrigation system to keep the plants alive. His philosophy about helping the community was quoted in the local newspapers, "If you promise someone you will help them, you don't say it in words, you do it in actions. You can't win them all but you certainly must try"

It took nine months from the time he brokered the deal with the county to realize the greening of several hundred feet. That was Phase One. He went forward with

Phase Two, which extended the Atlantic Avenue beautification project west of Jog Road toward the Turnpike. At a dinner in his honor many years later, the then mayor of Delray Beach, Thomas E. Lynch, said my father had set the example and "shamed" the city into beautifying the downtown area as well.

On a roll, my dad also talked the Village of Oriole's contractor into donating the model office to the Palm Beach County library system so they could open a West Delray branch. Upon his retirement as the president of the West Delray Democratic Club in 1992, a wooden plaque was erected in his honor on the median closest to that library branch. Whenever I call the Palm Beach County Parks and Recreation department, they always assure me that Jack's sign is well taken care of.

In His Footsteps

My father loved contributing to his new community and he definitely influenced me to do the same. With his example, it became second nature to me to make my community a better place to live. Wherever I move, I organize neighborhood get-togethers for everyone to get to know each other better. In North Carolina, I served on the Charlotte Community Relations Committee, and I have served on the board of Tryon's Friendship Council. When I was recently awarded membership in the Second Wind Hall of Fame for all of my work in the community, I knew my dad would be proud.

The West Delray Democratic Club

In keeping with his sense of service to his community and desire to help people, my dad became involved with the Atlantic Democratic Club shortly after he moved to Delray Beach. His father had served as a Democratic Party captain in the 6th Assembly District, and political hopefuls would come to his door for advice. Following in his father's footsteps, my dad said, "He always taught me to help people."

After the Atlantic Democratic Club split, he joined the Kings Point Democratic Club but, after a few meetings, he decided he was not happy with the way it was run (they probably were not making it happen fast enough for him). So, with the help of Jackie Malone, chairperson of the Democratic Executive Committee, he started his own club in 1978. What began with 35 people eventually mushroomed into the $1,800^+$-member West Delray Democratic Club political machine, also known as the WDDC.

Not one to stand around with his hands in his pockets, Dad liked to think of himself as an adopted ombudsman who helped others solve their problems with his political clout. Word quickly got out that, if Jack Babich couldn't fix it, he knew who could. The phone in their one-bedroom condo rang all day long with requests ranging from putting up a traffic light to adding a new bus route to trying to get out of a speeding ticket. The eternal problem-solver, my dad was in self-made heaven. My mother, on the other hand, insisted that they move to a two-bedroom apartment so he could receive his calls, and callers, in his office and she could have some peace and quiet in the rest of the house.

At the time, the county was divided into single-member districts with significant electoral clout and it did not take long for my dad to build the largest Democratic club in the state of Florida. Labeled the "Condo Czar" by the local newspapers, he was featured in the Wall Street Journal as an example of how retirees were making political waves. If candidates approached him for advice and he thought they had promise, he often campaigned for their election.

In addition to running meetings and organizing volunteers to collect dues and pass out notices, he became the editor of the WDDC newsletter. This gave him a far-reaching forum to get his opinions out beyond his membership. By now, almost all of the residents in the area knew of him and either loved him or hated him. As it goes in the political arena, he began making enemies as well as friends. That bothered him because he felt that he was out to help everybody.

After my mother's health took a turn for the worse, my dad decided to retire as President and hand over his gavel to a loyal WDDC member. The community gave him a huge send-off banquet. Among the 250 attendees, some of the local political luminaries that attended included Palm Beach County Commissioners Karen Marcus and Carol Roberts, State Senator Don Childers, State Representative Steve Press, and Delray Beach Mayor Doak Campbell. One of his fans, Richard L. Segum of Segum Industries, donated a large wooden sign to honor him and his contribution as an activist and President of WDDC for the Atlantic Avenue Beautification. It is still there today, installed on a median on Atlantic Avenue near the community library branch he had brokered to establish.

In His Footsteps

Shortly after Dad's retirement, I moved my family from Tampa to Delray Beach to fulfill my promise to be my mother's caregiver. After she passed away, Dad tried to convince me to get into politics by running for the school board. I felt I had spent too much time away from my family and did not take him up on it at the time. I did, however, work as an assistant for Palm Beach County Commissioner, Burt Aaronson, for a while and, since retiring, have worked diligently during each election season doing phone banking to get out the vote.

Building Friendships with Advice

As more and more independent roadside vendors dotted the byways selling hot dogs, fruits and vegetables, and flowers, their stands were becoming road hazards. Palm Beach County decided to require permits that set certain safety parameters, such as distance from the road and from each other. Eventually, the county added a dress code forcing the bikini-clad "babes" selling hot dogs to cover up and remain behind their carts to prevent rubberneckers from causing accidents.

After all of Dad's work to beautify the medians on West Atlantic Avenue, local officials had the impression that Jack Babich was the do-it-now, make-it-happen kind of guy to handle permit applications for the many roadside vendors. Herb Kahlert of the Palm Beach County engineering department created and offered him a part-time job as a vendor-compliance officer.

Making friends with many of the vendors, Dad often brought home past-their-peak bouquets and day-old hot dogs that could not be sold the next day. In exchange, he gave the curbside entrepreneurs advice about how to increase their business. When one family approached him for a license to open a fruit and vegetable stand, he urged them to sell only the best quality merchandise and to give away free samples. They took his advice to heart and The Boys Farmer's Market eventually became one of the most successful enterprises of its kind in the area.

Dad kept up his part-time job with the county for several years until he "retired" at age 79. (He actually did this to spend more time as the 11-year president and founder of the West Delray Democratic Club.) But that didn't stop him from checking in with his old friends along the roadside. They still valued his friendship and advice, and always greeted him with good cheer and the occasional handout.

In His Footsteps

Throughout my career helping people by facilitating life writing and forgiveness workshops, I enjoyed being able to offer advice when appropriate. Although the rewards didn't come in the form of hotdogs or flowers, I have enjoyed the sense of camaraderie and friendship that work gave me.

Bipartisan Politics

Photo by Jeff Greene, Palm Beach Post staff photographer, February 27, 1991

Although my dad was a Yellow Dog Democrat, he admired and befriended many Republican officials that he worked with during his tenure as president of the West Delray Democratic Club. He was known as the "King Maker" because many aspiring for political office sought his advice and approval. Such was the case when he endorsed Steve Press when he ran for South County Representative and campaigned for Burt Aaronson when he ran for Palm Beach County Commissioner.

Former Senator Robert Wexler, who served in the Florida Senate from 1990 to 1996 before being elected to the U.S. House of Representatives in 1996, was one of my dad's protégés. When Wexler decided to run for Congress, my dad discouraged him saying he was too young and would be eaten up alive. He ran anyway and was re-elected five times, until he resigned to become executive director of the Center for Middle East Peace and Economic Cooperation, a Washington-based think tank.

From the time I was able to make a difference at the polls with my vote, my Dad taught me how to draw conclusions about someone's political worth by scrutinizing their voting records. He did this for members of both parties. I was reminded of this credo many years after he passed away when I saw a 1947 movie called "The Farmer's Daughter." Loretta Young won Best Actress for her role in this film as a young woman who, after leaving her family's farm to study nursing in the city, finds herself on an unexpected path towards politics. During a debate, her character stood up in the audience and called out an unscrupulous candidate about his voting record. She eventually was tapped to run for office herself and went to Washington, a scenario my father would have loved to see come true for me.

When it was no longer safe for Dad to drive, I used to chauffeur him to various political events where he would introduce me to state and county officials from both parties. Although he glad-handed them to their faces, on the way home I would invariably get an earful about their long suits and shortcomings. He would say something like, "He's such a nice guy but the poor schmo will never get elected." I would also hear, "That bastard so-and-so didn't vote for such-and-such, even after he promised he would when he ran for office." He even sometimes admitted, "I wish we had more Republicans like him that vote for what's best for the people."

In His Footsteps

Alas, I disappointed my Dad with my non-political ambitions. However, I have been stalwart in my instruction to vote according to the person's record, even in today's "us against them" political climate. I spent time as an organizer for Braver Angels, the organization that runs workshops, debates, and other events where "red" and "blue" participants attempt to better understand one another's positions and discover their shared values. My dad would have loved to be a part of those conversations.

Use It Up

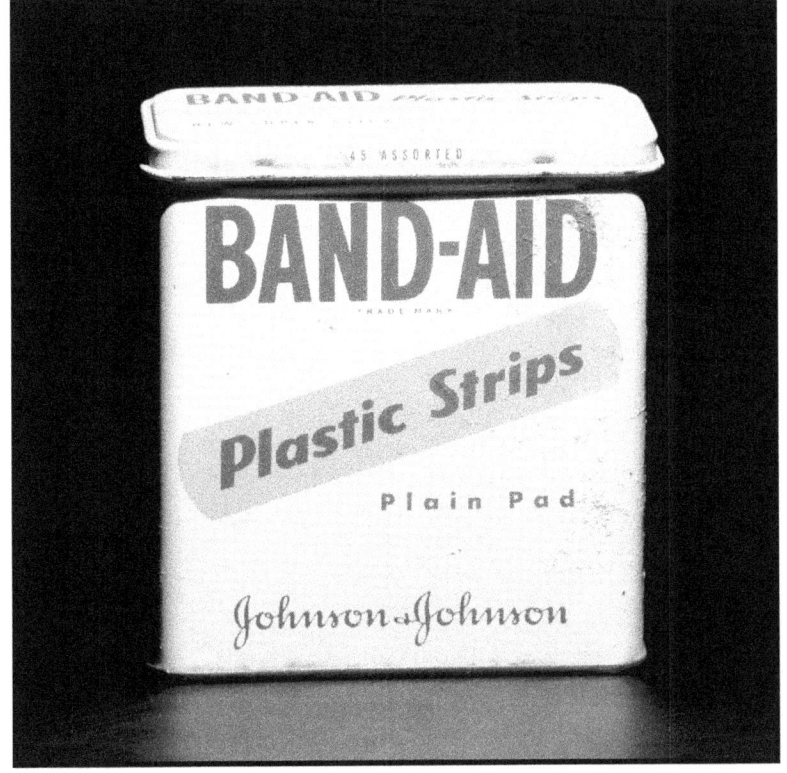

Once my mom was gone and my dad no longer had political duties to attend to, I became a sounding board for his opinions and suggestions. Most of the time, I would only half listen because I was convinced I had heard it all before. Over the years, in spite of myself, some of them stuck with me.

"Use it up," was the dictum my father would pronounce if I ever wanted to throw something away that he thought could still be of service. Some of that mentality may have been due to him growing up during the Great Depression. I also believe he "came out of the factory" with a little bit more of a compulsion to save the world from waste than how most of us are wired.

Throughout his condominium, you could find examples of this credo. An envelope from opened mail became a scratch pad for phone messages, and old Band-Aid boxes were perfect containers for paperclips. Whatever was falling apart often gained a new lease on life with generously applied scotch tape. File folders in his office that were worn to a pulp were bandaged with enough tape to make them waterproof.

My father's use it up philosophy had also worn off on my mother. In her kitchen, aluminum foil was never a single-use item. It was washed, folded neatly, and stored for the next usage such as catching drippings in the toaster oven or lining kitchen drawers. Clothing that she could no longer mend became rags for cleaning.

Sometimes, Dad took things a little too far, like continuing to wear sneakers that were too small so he felt that he had gotten his money's worth out of them. He also would rummage through the refrigerator and make sandwiches with food that was dated way past its prime saying, "A little dab of mustard or horseradish goes a long way!"

In His Footsteps

Growing up with his example, the habit of repurposing must have become ingrained in me. I believe what I learned from my father's penchant to avoid waste has been put to good use with the grassroots organization I started called "Generations Against Single-Use Plastic" (G.A.S.P.). I give presentations about plastic pollution solutions for civic organizations and libraries. In the schools, I'm often joined by my husband, David who is an artist working with recyclable plastic containers like shampoo and detergent bottles. He will often follow my talk with a workshop on how to make jellyfish from water bottles or butterflies from yogurt containers. Together, we are keeping my dad's use it up legacy alive!

Pieces of String
and Pennies from Heaven

After my father passed away, I had the task of cleaning out my parents' condo in order to put it up for sale. Although I knew he had a hard time discarding things, I was still amazed at what I found in his closet. Among the hodgepodge of used nails, screws, and rubber bands, there were the old knobs from their kitchen cabinets – some of them broken – that he had replaced 20 years ago. There were also no less than five unopened boxes of aluminum foil that he probably could not resist buying when they went on sale.

Born in 1910, one might chalk his hoarding up to the fact that he was a young man during the Great Depression, but I knew better. He just could not bear to see something thrown away that might still be useful. On our many outings together after my mother was gone, he would meticulously scan the pavement, looking for the odd piece of string or a half-used pencil. Stooping to pick up some treasure, he would instruct me with, "You never know when this will come in handy." He especially loved to search parking lots for stray coins. No matter how large or small his find, he always beamed from ear to ear.

I heard a funny story from one of the owners of the family outdoor fruit stand that my father helped to get established in Delray Beach. He said he would often toss some coins out in his parking lot when he saw my father's car pull up to their outdoor fruit and vegetable stand. It gave the owner such a kick to see my father's face light up with pleasure. He said, "Your dad never knew that they were not pennies from heaven."

In His Footsteps

Finding money on the street is often considered a symbol of unexpected good fortune or luck. It can also be seen as a sign of abundance and a reminder to be grateful for the blessings in your life. Although I do not take after my father's propensity to pick up items in the street, I do often take time to scan a parking lot for stray coins. When I find one, I hold it up and say, "This one's for you, Dad."

Leaving a Legacy

South County Civic Center (Photo: Palm Beach County Parks and Recreation Department)

My dad worked tirelessly, for years, to get Palm Beach County to build a civic center in his district. He felt there was a need for public meetings and recreational programming for the residents in the area. Once he proposed the concept, he sat through meeting after meeting to get the county commissioners to approve it and decide on a location. They finally picked the corner of Jog-Carter and Morikami Park Roads. Although my Dad also tried to get the county commissioners to name it after my mom, in honor of her unsung support to the community, that motion did not pass.

Regardless of his disappointment that it did not carry on my mother's name, the Center was still a wonderful legacy about my father's sense of and dedication to his community. Former Palm Beach County Commissioner, Karen Roberts, summed it up when she said, "Jack Babich did for the community as much as any mayor or any commissioner can do."

Today, the South County Civic Center is a bevy of activity and a huge success. Located on a five-acre tract, it has a 500-seat auditorium with a stage and can be subdivided to accommodate smaller meetings and recreational activities. It also has two classrooms and a food distribution area for serving the community.

In His Footsteps

My husband and I enjoy walking along the Vaughn Creek Greenway in the outskirts of Tryon with our little dog, Bonnie. A few years after it was opened, we volunteered to be trail stewards to monitor the walkway and inform the Tryon Parks committee of any problems such as a downed limb or overflowing sewage. I also campaigned, like my dad, for several years to donate two benches so others who were enjoying the walkway could sit and rest and enjoy the ambiance of the flowing water and cascading falls. With the help of Terry Ackerman, one of the committee members, we finally achieved that goal. Terry liked the idea so much that he and Monica Jones actually purchased three more benches to place along the way. So many people have thanked me for this small gesture over the years, especially those with back problems or Parkinson's who need that respite to continue.

Finding Memories
to Footsteps

Whose footsteps do you follow? In my reminiscence workshops, I help people find the significant people and events that shaped their lives by having them follow their senses. The sense of smell, like fresh baked bread or a certain perfume, is the strongest. It triggers memories because the nerve endings from the nose go directly to the part of the brain that holds most memories. Sounds, old photos, or objects can also help you remember the past.

Write down the first thing that comes to mind and start your story with where you are and whom you are with. Describe what you are doing and how you feel. Before long, even a sentence or two can grow into a story. If you get stuck, share the story with others as the details often appear in the process of conversation.

Not all memories may be happy ones. If that's the case, you may be able to find the laughter looking back on it with adult eyes. You can also look for any life lessons you learned from negative experiences. It took more than my wet footprints on a bathmat for me to recognize how Dad's life influenced my own. I hope my recollections about my Dad inspire you to do the same. Maybe you have another family member or acquaintance whose actions made a lasting impression on you. When you answer some of the questions on the following pages, they may trigger memories that will enable you to determine whose footsteps you follow.

Is there a certain place you put your keys or loose change?

What was your favorite food as a child? Do you remember when you first ate it and whom you were with?

When you celebrate a holiday, do you follow a tradition that was handed down by a family member?

Have you ever caught yourself repeating a phrase your father or another loved one used?

_____
_____
_____
_____
_____
_____
_____
_____
_____
_____
_____
_____
_____
_____
_____
_____

Acknowledgements

Teaching the healing power of reminiscence over the past 25 years, I have helped so many people recognize the significant people and events that shaped their lives. Looking back on my own life, I saw how fortunate I was to grow up with the influence of both of my parents who taught me by their example to do what I loved to do, do it well, and, most importantly, to help people along the way.

I actually started *In My Father's Footsteps* about ten years ago, thinking it would be a natural sequel to my first book, *In My Mother's Kitchen*, and a way to celebrate fathers. Distracted by other books and projects, it slept in my file cabinet, unfinished, until I had the opportunity to read the initial and newer stories for this book at the Upstairs Artspace Literary Night in Tryon, North Carolina. Hoping to see if there was any merit in finishing it, I was delighted by the encouragement from the other writers and listeners present. No matter how many books I have written and edited, I found it a bit daunting to proceed. Thankfully, David Adelman, my talented son, agreed to do the layout to complete this project. Then, my new friend, Maggie Powell, came into my life just in time to do the final editing. As always, my husband and life partner, David Edgar, continued to be my cheerleader to do what I loved to do. Hopefully, the end result of our collaboration to bring you *In My Father's Footsteps* has helped you, too!

About the Author

Robin A. Edgar is a retired professional journalist. She now conducts reminiscence-writing workshops in a variety of venues, including schools and art centers such as the prestigious John C. Campbell Folk School in Brasstown, North Carolina. In addition, she teaches The Healing Power of Reminiscence workshop for caregiver organizations affiliated with National Hospice and Palliative Care and The Alzheimer's Association, and facilitates conversations for the Campaign for Love & Forgiveness, a project sponsored by the Fetzer Institute.

Ms. Edgar is the author of five other books: *In My Mother's Kitchen: An Introduction to the Healing Power of Reminiscence*; *Personal Legacies: Surviving the Great Depression*; *Fantastic Recycled Plastic*; *The Day Morris Quit*; and *The Day Morris Went to School*. She lives with her husband in Landrum, South Carolina.

Me and Dad

www.ingramcontent.com/pod-product-compliance
Lightning Source LLC
Chambersburg PA
CBHW062112290426

44110CB00023B/2791